Remarkable Landmarks

Our Great Lakes

by Dona Herweck Rice

Consultant
Cheryl Lane, M.Ed.
Classroom Teacher, California

Publishing Credits
Rachelle Cracchiolo, M.S.Ed., *Publisher*
Emily R. Smith, M.A.Ed., *SVP of Content Development*
Véronique Bos, *VP of Creative*
Dani Neiley, *Editor*
Kevin Pham, *Senior Graphic Designer*

Image Credits: p.1 Courtesy of NASA; pp.6–7 AI_Firefly; p.10 Istockphoto/Atlantic-kid; all other images from iStock and/or Shutterstock

This book has been filed with the Library of Congress.
LCCN: 2026020103
ISBN: 979-8-3309-2994-8

TCM Teacher Created Materials
5482 Argosy Avenue
Huntington Beach, CA 92649
www.tcmpub.com

Printed by 51250
PO 22957 / Printed in USA

TABLE OF CONTENTS

WHAT MAKES A LANDMARK SPECIAL OR UNIQUE?

Landmarks help tell the story of a place. Some are made by people, such as tall towers and famous BRIDGES. Others are made by nature, such as mighty mountains or deep canyons. Landmarks stand out. They are special because they show us something unique about our world.

Landmarks serve a few purposes. They can remind us of history. They can honor culture. Or they can reveal the power of nature. When we learn about them, we find ways that people and the planet are connected.

Have you ever visited a place that felt unforgettable to you? That feeling might be because you found a landmark—one that makes its mark on the world.

Great Lakes, United States and Canada

Wow-Worthy Wonders

Some landmarks can even be seen from space—like the Great Lakes!

Mount Fitz Roy, Argentina

London Bridge, England

A NATURAL WONDER

Have you ever stood beside a lake **so big** you couldn't see the other side? That's what it feels like to visit the Great Lakes. They are nature's **masterpiece**!

There are five lakes among the Great Lakes. They are so large that they look like oceans. They hold about one-fifth of all the **fresh water** on Earth! They touch both the United States and Canada.

Together, the lakes form one of the most important landmarks in North America. They connect people, animals, and places. Ships travel their waters, carrying goods across the miles. Fish, birds, and other wildlife depend on the lakes for food and shelter. People explore, work, and play along their shores every day.

That's Superior!

There is so much water in Lake Superior that it could cover all the land of North and South America in a foot of water!

The Big Five

The five Great Lakes are called Huron, Ontario, Michigan, Erie, and Superior. Some people remember them by their first letters, which spell HOMES.

Lake Superior

Fun Fact: This is the largest and deepest of the lakes.

Size: 31,700 square miles (82,100 square kilometers) and 1,333 feet (406 meters) deep

Lake Michigan

Fun Fact: Some sand dunes along its shores are taller than many buildings.

Size: 22,300 square miles (57,760 square kilometers) and 923 feet (281 meters) deep

GREAT LAKES AT A GLANCE

The Great Lakes may be best known for their size. They are about equal in size to the whole United Kingdom!

They were formed thousands of years ago by melting **glaciers**. The lakes are connected by rivers and smaller lakes that lead to the Atlantic Ocean.

Lake Huron

Fun Fact: This lake is home to more than 30,000 islands.

Size: 23,000 square miles (59,570 square kilometers) and 750 feet (229 meters) deep

Lake Ontario

Fun Fact: This is the smallest of the lakes by surface area. It also connects the lakes to the Atlantic Ocean.

Size: 7,300 square miles (18,910 square kilometers) and 802 feet (244 meters) deep

Lake Erie

Fun Fact: Because of its shallow water, Lake Erie sometimes freezes over in winter.

Size: 9,900 square miles (25,640 square kilometers) and 210 feet (64 meters) deep

THE GREAT LAKES THROUGH TIME

The Great Lakes have changed over thousands of years. From icy beginnings to busy cities, their story is always flowing. Take a look at how these mighty lakes have grown and changed through time.

20,000 years ago—Melting glaciers fill the deep basins of the Great Lakes with fresh water.

8,000 years ago—**Indigenous** peoples live along the lakes.

1600s—Early explorers use the lakes as travel routes through North America.

1800s—Settlers build towns and shipping ports along the coasts. Large ships begin carrying goods across the lakes.

1900s—Factories and cities are built. People start to notice pollution problems.

1972—Leaders from the United States and Canada sign an agreement to protect and clean up the Great Lakes.

Today—Millions of people live, work, and play near and on the Great Lakes. The story of the Great Lakes is still being written—by all of us!

A Place Called Home

The Great Lakes have long been a sacred place for Indigenous peoples. Many nations have lived in this area throughout history. They include the Haudenosanee, Anishinaabe, and more.

members of the Anishinaabe, 1962

City Life

Major cities like Chicago, Cleveland, and Toronto grew up next to the Great Lakes. Why do you think that is?

LIFE AROUND THE LAKES

People have built their lives along the Great Lakes for thousands of years. Today, big cities BUZZ WITH LIFE beside the water. Ships carry food, cars, and supplies across the lakes. Families fish, swim, and play on sandy shores. Millions of tourists visit the lakes each year! They come from around the world.

The lakes are also home to forests, **wetlands**, and countless creatures. People and wildlife share this WATERY world side by side. Trout swim below the waves. Eagles soar above. Beavers build their homes along the edges. And mayflies start their lives below water before taking to the skies.

SEASONS OF CHANGE

When spring arrives, **MELTING ICE** fills the streams. The water supports new life. Fish swim upriver, and plants begin to bloom.

The Great Lakes never stay the same for long. In winter, **ICY WINDS** freeze the edges of the lakes. Snow piles high along the shores. Some animals rest or move to warmer places.

Summer WARMS the water. Boats are a constant sight on the lakes. People swim, sail, and fish across the region.

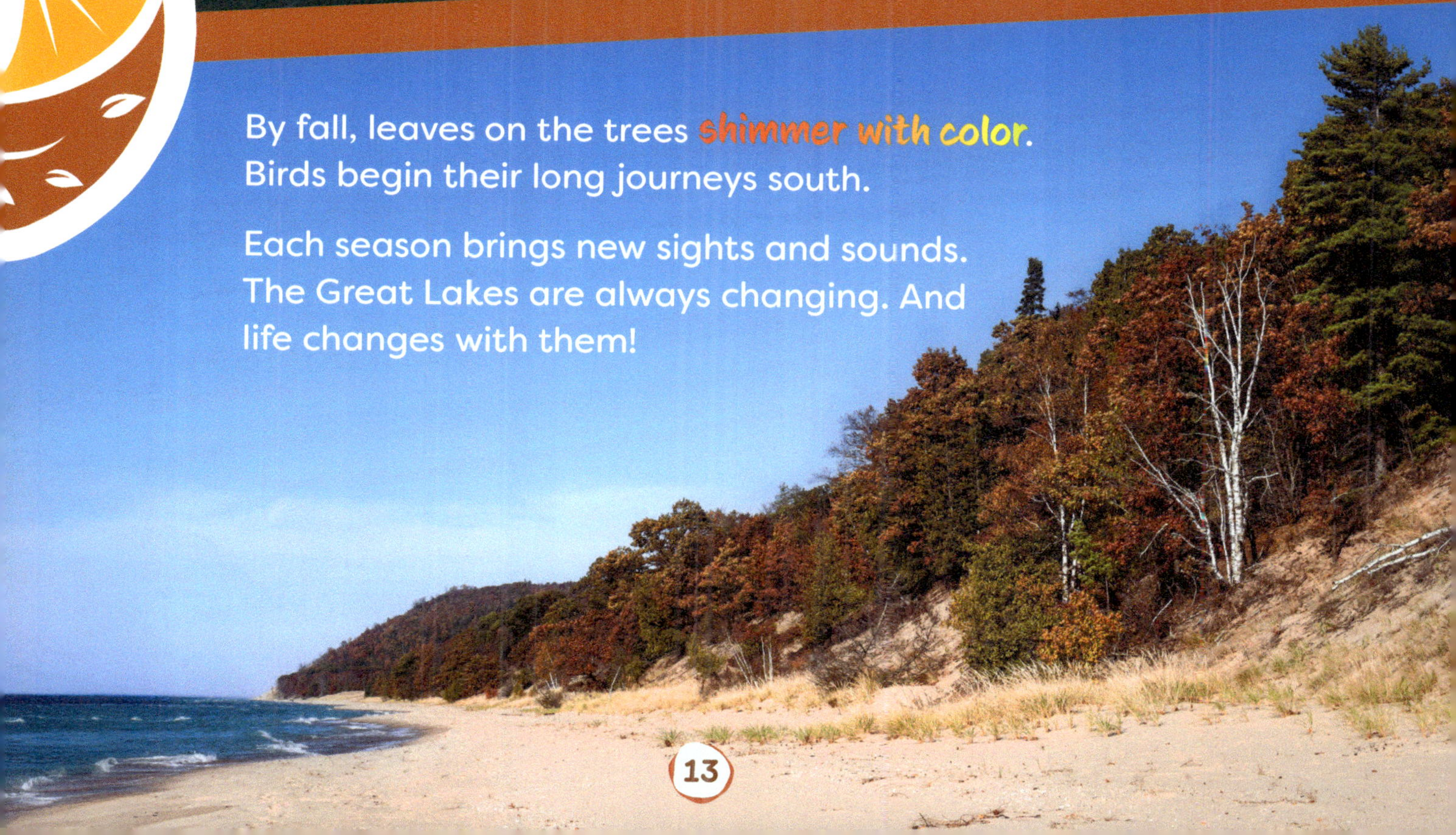

By fall, leaves on the trees shimmer with color. Birds begin their long journeys south.

Each season brings new sights and sounds. The Great Lakes are always changing. And life changes with them!

A DIFFERENT VIEW

The Great Lakes are part of a massive **waterway** system. Take a look!

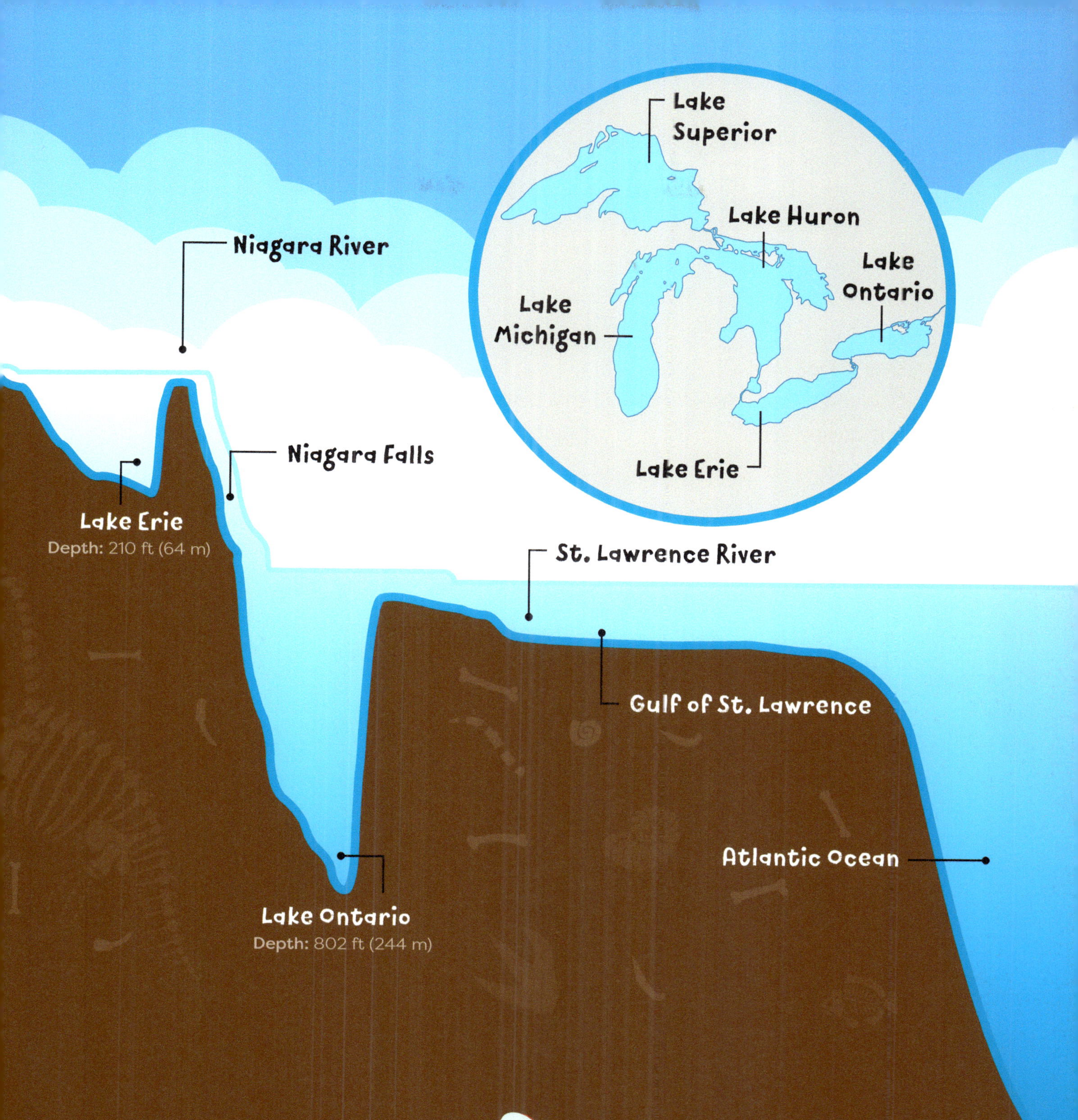
Lake Superior
Lake Huron
Lake Ontario
Lake Michigan
Lake Erie
Niagara River
Niagara Falls
Lake Erie
Depth: 210 ft (64 m)
St. Lawrence River
Gulf of St. Lawrence
Atlantic Ocean
Lake Ontario
Depth: 802 ft (244 m)

PROTECTING OUR GREAT LAKES

The Great Lakes give people and animals clean water, food, and fun. But the lakes need care to stay healthy. Trash, chemicals, and too much waste can **pollute** the water. **Invasive** plants and animals harm **native** species. The changing climate brings warmer water and stronger storms.

But there's good news. People are taking action! Scientists study the water and discover ways to help. Volunteers clean up beaches.

Leaders create laws to help protect wildlife and keep pollution out.

Every effort counts. **Conservation** of the lakes helps every living thing that depends on them. And it protects the lakes for the future.

Tiny Trouble

Zebra mussels are an invasive species. They are small creatures, but they cause big problems. They clog pipes and harm native fish.

YOU CAN MAKE A DIFFERENCE

Even the smallest actions can make a big impact. Turning off the faucet while brushing your teeth saves gallons of water. Picking up litter keeps it from washing into storm drains, which lead to lakes, rivers, and oceans. Choosing reusable bottles reduces plastic trash and keeps it out of the lakes.

You can also learn more and share what you know with others. When many people take SMALL steps, they add up to BIG changes! Everyone can help keep our lakes clean, safe, and full of life.

A Long Time

One plastic bottle can take hundreds of years to break down in water!

THE LAKES OF TOMORROW

The story of the Great Lakes isn't finished. It's still being written every day! Around the lakes, people are using new ideas to protect the water. Cities are building gardens that collect and filter rain before it reaches the lakes. Farmers are planting cover crops to keep soil and chemicals from washing away. Engineers are inventing filters that clean stormwater before it flows back to nature.

Global Wonder

The Great Lakes are the largest group of freshwater lakes on Earth.

These efforts show what can happen when people and science work together. By caring for nature, we care for our future. The Great Lakes belong to everyone. Protecting them makes sure that generations to come will be able to enjoy them, too.

A LIVING LANDMARK

The Great Lakes are one of Earth's great treasures. They hold stories of people, animals, and nature working together. Their rolling waves meet busy cities and thriving forests alike. The lakes give us water to drink and food to eat. Perhaps best of all, they offer great beauty for everyone to enjoy.

Every drop of WATER connects life, from tiny insects to soaring eagles. When we explore the Great Lakes, we explore a living landmark. Their story is part of *our* story, too.

Water for Everyone

About 35 million people get their drinking water from the Great Lakes!

AROUND THE WORLD

Our planet is full of amazing bodies of water. Each one is special in its own way. Some are deep and ancient. Others are wide and wild. Together, they shape life on Earth, just like the Great Lakes do. Explore these watery wonders from around the world!

Lake Baikal

Russia

This is the deepest lake in the world! It holds one-fifth of Earth's fresh water. It is home to animals found nowhere else on Earth, such as the Baikal seal.

The Amazon River

South America

This is the second-longest river on Earth. It flows through rainforests and carries more water than any other river in the world.

The Dead Sea

Middle East

This is a saltwater lake. The lake is so salty that people can float easily on its surface! It is one of the lowest places on land, sitting far below sea level.

Lake Victoria

Africa

This is Africa's largest lake and the world's second-largest freshwater lake. It is shared by three countries. The lake is home to hundreds of fish species.

The Great Barrier Reef

Australia

This is a massive coral reef system that is found in shallow lagoons along Australia's coast. It is the world's largest living structure. It is so big that it can be seen from space.

Lake Titicaca

South America

This is the highest **navigable** lake in the world. It is surrounded by mountains. It is home to many floating islands made of reeds.

JUST FOR YOU

You don't have to live near the Great Lakes to explore and protect water! Here are some fun things to do to learn, create, and make a difference, right where you are.

Lake Detective

Flip through *Our Great Lakes* again and see what you can spot! How many boats can you find in the pictures? What about fish and birds?

Water Walk

Go for a walk near a pond, stream, or even a puddle. What do you see living or growing in or near the water?

Lake Experiment

Fill a clear bowl with water and drop in small twigs, leaves, or pebbles. Watch what floats and what sinks. How do you think wind, rain, or waves might move these objects around in a real lake?

Sound of the Shore

When you're near water, close your eyes and listen. What water sounds can you hear? A splash, drip, or wave? Try making your own lake "music" by tapping, sloshing, and swooshing!

Lake Promise

Write or draw one way you can help keep water clean—such as using less plastic, turning off the tap, or sharing what you learned.

GLOSSARY

conservation—a careful preservation and protection of something

fresh water—of, relating to, or living in water that is not salty

glaciers—very large areas of ice that move slowly down slopes or valleys or over wide areas of land

Indigenous—inhabiting or existing in a land from the earliest times or before settlers arrived

invasive—tending to spread and create harm

landmarks—objects or structures on land that are easy to see or recognize and may be important in history

masterpiece—a great work of art or something created with great skill

native—made or living naturally in a particular area

navigable—deep and wide enough to allow ships to travel

waterway—a body of water that is deep and wide enough for boats and ships to travel through

wetlands—areas of land that are covered with shallow water, such as marshes or swamps

INDEX

BE CURIOUS

1. What makes the Great Lakes worth exploring and protecting?
2. How do people, animals, and plants depend on the Great Lakes?
3. How do the changing seasons shape life in and around the Great Lakes?
4. How can you help protect the Great Lakes and other natural landmarks near you?

ABOUT THE AUTHOR

Dona Herweck Rice has written hundreds of books, stories, and poems for kids on just about every topic under the sun, from acrobats to zucchini and everything in between. Writing is her passion, but she also loves reading, live theater, dancing anytime and anywhere, and singing at the top of her lungs. She thinks lake life is one of the best things there is, and the Great Lakes are one of the most spectacular places on Earth.

Dona was a teacher and is an acting coach. She lives in southern California with her husband, son, and one cute, silly, and loveable little dog.